What's the Weather Today?

By Allan Fowler

Consultants:
Robert L. Hillerich, Ph.D., Bowling Green
State University, Bowling Green, Ohio

Mary Nalbandian, Director of Science,
Chicago Public Schools, Chicago, Illinois

Fay Robinson, Child Development Specialist

CHILDREN'S PRESS
A Division of Grolier Publishing
Sherman Turnpike
Danbury, Connecticut 06816

Series cover and interior design by Sara Shelton

Library of Congress Cataloging-in-Publication Data

Fowler, Allan.
    What's the weather today? / by Allan Fowler.
      p. cm. —(Rookie read-about science)
    Summary: A simple explanation of weather and climate.
    ISBN 0-516-04918-6
    1. Weather—Juvenile literature. 2. Climate—Juvenile literature.
  [1.Weather. 2. Climate] I. Title. II. Series: Fowler, Allan.
    Rookie read-about science.
QC981.3.F68 1991
551.6—dc20
                           91-3125
                            CIP
                            AC

On your way to school today, did you feel hot or cold? Or just in-between?

Was it sunny or cloudy?

Raining or snowing or dry?

Was it windy?

All those things are part of weather.

Weather often changes from one day to the next. It could even change a lot during a single day.

9

Sometimes you wear a rain coat to school because it's raining in the morning, or it looks like rain. But on your way home, it's bright and sunny!

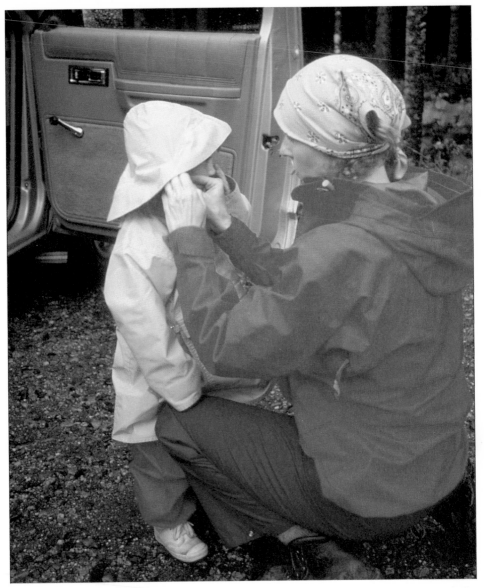

The weather also depends on where you live. In many places, each season has a different kind of weather.

Winter is cold...

spring is warmer...

summer is hot...

and fall is cooler.

There are other places where it's warm most of the time, and it never, never snows. (Well, hardly ever.)

18

And there are places where it's cold all the time.

You have to dress like this to keep warm.

When it rains so hard
that you can't go out
and play, you might think
the weather is bad.

But this farmer thinks
it's good. The crops need
rain to grow.

People called meteorologists
tell us what kind of
weather we might have
later in the day...

and tomorrow...and the
day after tomorrow.

They warn us when a big storm is coming, so we can stay inside and be safe.

Can you guess what the weather will be like later today?

Try it!

Just step outside, feel the air, and look up at the sky and the clouds. Now...
do you think it will rain?

Words You Know

weather

sunny

cloudy

snowing

raining

windy

seasons

winter

spring

summer

fall

hot weather

cold weather

storm

sky and clouds

Index

About the Author

Allan Fowler is a free-lance writer with a background in advertising. Born in New York, he lives in Chicago now and enjoys traveling.

Photo Credits

Photo courtesy of The National Broadcasting Company, Inc.—© Al Levine, 25

PhotoEdit—© Myrleen Ferguson, 6, 13, 16, 31 (top left and right)

TSW-CLICK/Chicago—© Norbert Nu, 17

Valan—© Stephen Krasemann, Cover; © Irwin Barrett, 4; © J. Bruneau, 5, 21, 30 (center left); © V. Wilkinson, 28; © Pierre Kohler, 9, 31 (bottom left); © Jane K. Hugesson, 11; © Francis Lépine, 15, 30 (center right), 31 (top center right); © V. Whelan, 31 (center left); © Anthony Scullion, 18; © Don McPhee, 22; © Dennis Schmidt, 26; © Kennon Cooke, 30 (top left); © Harold V. Green, 30 (top right); © Chris Malazdrewicz, 30 (bottom right); © Michel Julien, 31 (center right); © R. LaSalle, 31 (bottom right)

© Jim Whitmer—14, 31 (top center left)

COVER: Rainbow, Alaska